TRIANGLES

Shapes in Math, Science and Nature

Written by Catherine Sheldrick Ross
Illustrated by Bill Slavin

Kids Can Press Ltd.
Toronto

Kids Can Press Ltd. acknowledges with appreciation the assistance of the Canada Council and the Ontario Arts Council in the production of this book.

Canadian Cataloguing in Publication Data

Ross, Catherine Sheldrick
    Triangles: shapes in math, science and nature

Includes index.
ISBN 1-55074-194-2

1. Triangle — Juvenile literature. I. Slavin, Bill.
II. Title.

QA482.R67 1994   j516'.15   C94-931173-1

Kids Can Press Ltd.
29 Birch Avenue
Toronto, Ontario, Canada
M4V 1E2

Edited by Laurie Wark
Designed by Esperança Melo
Printed and bound in Canada

94 0 9 8 7 6 5 4 3 2 1

 Text stock contains
over 50% recycled paper

Contents

Acknowledgements

Once again, thanks are due to many people. Hugh Kenner's book *Bucky: A Guided Tour of Buckminster Fuller* first got me interested in tensegrity forms made out of triangles, but Bruce Ross went one step further and built them. Kenneth Fruh of the Philadelphia Fire Department provided useful information about the department's fire hydrant design. Kay McKenzie, mayor of the Town of Vegreville, gave helpful answers to my questions about Vegreville's famous Pysanka. Professor Douglas Edge of the Faculty of Education, University of Western Ontario, read the manuscript and made helpful suggestions. And thank you, folks at Kids Can Press: Laurie Wark for her editorial genius and tact; Esperança Melo for her book design; and Bill Slavin for the engaging illustrations.

Introduction

Have you ever noticed how many interesting things come in threes? There are the three little pigs, the three Musketeers, the three Wise Men, three wishes and "three strikes — you're out." In fairy tales, it's third time lucky. When you hear "Once upon a time, a woodcutter had three sons," you know that the third son will cut down the magic tree, find the treasure inside and live happily ever after. Think of tricycles, triceratops, Napoleon's tricorn hat, the trillium, the three-leaf clover and, of course, the triangle, with three sides and three angles.

Triangles are flat — they have only two dimensions. But if you put four triangular sides, or faces, together into a closed shape, you get a tetrahedron. Take a flat triangle and stretch it up to give it some thickness, and you have a triangular prism shape, like the prism that Newton used to split light into the colours of the rainbow. Arrange four triangular sides onto a square base, and you get a pyramid shape, like the great Egyptian pyramids.

When you read *Triangles*, you'll find out how triangles are used to measure heights and distances, make some mind-bending puzzles to wow your friends, discover why builders can't get along without triangles, learn about Alexander Graham Bell's tetrahedral kites, make a kaleidoscope, grow a crystal with eight triangular faces and much more.

If you find a triangle word you don't understand, check the glossary on page 62 for an explanation.

1 Amazing Triangles

Three dots are all you need to make a triangle. Just make sure the dots you draw are not in a straight line and then connect the dots. As you can see, triangles have three sides and three angles. Triangles are simple, elegant and strong and turn up when you least expect them. The triangle spider weaves her web into a triangular shape. The desert tortoise grows its shell in a hexagonal pattern made from six triangles.

That's why they're called tri-angles — **tri** is the Greek word for "three."

Making triangles

Find out about different kinds of triangles by making some from strips of cardboard and paper fasteners. When you're finished, save the cardboard strips for finding out about angles (see page 10) and for testing out your engineering savvy (see page 36).

You'll need:
Bristol board in three different colours
a ruler
a pencil
scissors
a one-hole punch
a package of paper fasteners

1. From one colour of Bristol board, cut at least ten strips that are 9 cm (3 inches) long and about 1 cm (1/3 inch) wide.

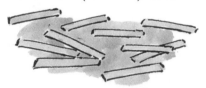

2. From a second colour of Bristol board, cut at least ten strips that are 12 cm (4 inches) long and about 1 cm (1/3 inch) wide.

3. From a third colour of Bristol board, cut at least ten strips that are 15 cm (5 inches) long and about 1 cm (1/3 inch) wide.

4. Use the one-hole punch to make holes at each end of the Bristol board strips.

5. Make some triangles from three strips joined together with the paper fasteners. How many different triangles can you make, without making the same-sized triangle twice?

With these strips, you can make ten different triangles. Three of the triangles are equilateral triangles, with three sides of the same length. These three triangles are similar triangles, which means they have the same shape, although they are different sizes. You can make six different triangles that have two sides of the same length. They are called isosceles triangles. And you can make one triangle with sides of three different lengths. It is called a scalene triangle.

Take a closer look at the three kinds of triangles you just made.

Equilateral triangle
All three sides of this triangle are the same length.

Isosceles triangle
Two sides of this triangle are the same length.

Scalene triangle
The sides of this triangle are all different lengths.

You can't make a triangle from just any three strips of paper. The length of any one side must be shorter than the length of the other two sides added together or it won't work. Check this out for yourself—try making a triangle with two sides of 8 cm (3 inches) and one side of 20 cm (8 inches).

Keeping in shape with triangles

You can make shapes with three, four, five, six, sixty or more sides. The triangle is the polygon, or closed flat shape, with the fewest sides. If you tried to make a closed shape with only two sides, all you would get is a V-shape with an open end.

Use your strips of paper and a paper fastener from the last activity (page 7) to make a V-shape. The sides of this V move around like the hands of a clock. But attach a third strip of paper and the sides become locked. Now push on the corners — the triangle keeps its shape. Each side prevents the angle opposite it from opening or closing.

You might think that if three sides are strong, four sides will be even stronger. Try it. Use paper fasteners to attach four strips together. Push on the corners. Hmmmm — the four-sided shape squashes flat. What if you add a diagonal strip to the four-sided shape? Now the angles are locked because you have turned your four-sided shape into two triangles.

Do you think more sides will help? Try making a pentagon (a five-sided figure) or a hexagon (six-sided). As you see, adding more sides doesn't help. The triangle is the only polygon that keeps its shape under pressure.

Polygon comes from two Greek words — **poly**, meaning "many," and **gon**, meaning "angles."

THE TRIANGLE UP CLOSE

A **vertex** is a point where two sides of a triangle meet.

An **altitude** is a line from one vertex that is at right angles, or perpendicular, to the opposite side.

The **base** is the bottom, or lowest side, of a triangle.

The **median** of a triangle is the straight line joining a vertex to a midpoint of the opposite side.

The **midpoint** is the point that divides a side into two equal parts.

You can figure out the distance around the outside of a triangle (its perimeter) by adding up the lengths of its three sides.

FIND THE HIDDEN TRIANGLES

To make this brain-teaser, all you need is a square of paper.

1. Fold the paper in half to make a triangle. Sharpen the crease by running your thumbnail over the fold line.

2. Fold the triangle in half, and fold again twice more to end up with a small folded triangle. Sharpen the crease each time.

3. When you unfold the paper, you'll see 16 small triangles that are all the same size. How many triangles can you find altogether? (Don't say 16.) (See page 64 for the answer.)

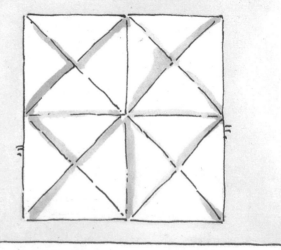

—9—

Angles

Geese do it when they fly in a V-formation. Trees do it when they branch. Scissors do it when they cut paper. Your arm does it when you bend it to lift something. What are all these things doing? Forming an angle. When two sides come together at one point, they form an angle.

The angles of a triangle come in lots of shapes. Experiment with angles, using the V-shape (two strips of paper joined with a paper fastener) that you made on page 8.

1. Start with the unattached ends close together. This gives you an acute angle — an angle smaller than 90°.

2. Arrange the two strips to look like the two hands of a clock set to 12:15 P.M. — with one hand on the twelve and the other on the three. The angle you have made is a right angle, or a 90° angle.

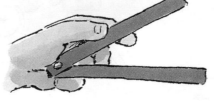

90°

3. Open up the strip a bit more — to look like the hands of a clock set to 12:20 or 12:25 P.M. Now you have an obtuse angle, which is any angle greater than 90° and less than 180°. (An angle of 180° is a straight line and is called a straight angle.)

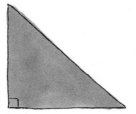

If you sort triangles according to the lengths of their sides, you've already discovered that you get equilateral, isosceles and scalene triangles. But if you sort them according to the sizes of their angles, you get acute triangles, right triangles and obtuse triangles.

Acute triangle
Each of the angles measures less than 90°.

Right triangle
Has an angle of 90°.

Obtuse triangle
Has an angle measuring more than 90°.

Adding up the angles

3. Rip off the corners of the triangle.

What would you call a triangle having both a right angle and an obtuse angle? You'd call it impossible. See for yourself.

You'll need:
paper
a pencil
a ruler
scissors
3 crayons or coloured markers of different
  colours

1. Draw a triangle on the paper and cut it out.

2. Colour each angle a different colour.

4. Fit the three corners together around a single point. What do you get?

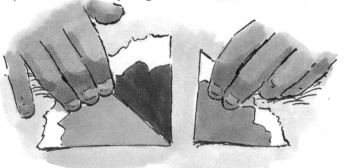

5. Do you think it was just lucky that you ended up with a straight line? Try it again with a differently shaped triangle.

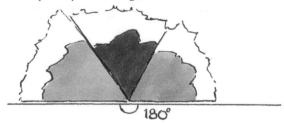

180°

What's happening?
The three angles inside a triangle will always sit together on a straight line. No matter what sizes the three angles are, they always add up to 180°, which is a straight line. That's why you can't have a triangle with both a right angle and an obtuse angle—these angles would add up to more than 180°.

Cutting the angles in half

Cut out a paper triangle and fold one of the angles through its vertex so that the sides touch. When you unfold it, you can see that the fold line now bisects the angle, or divides it into two equal parts. Here's another way to bisect an angle.

You'll need:
paper
a pencil
a ruler
a compass

1. Draw any angle ABC with sides at least 7 cm (3 inches) long.

2. Open your compass to about 6 cm (21/2 inches). Put the compass foot on the vertex of the angle and draw arcs to cut the sides at D and E.

3. Put the compass foot on D and draw an arc as shown. Put the compass foot on E and draw a second arc to intersect or cut across the first arc at F.

4. The line BF bisects the angle ABC, dividing it in half.

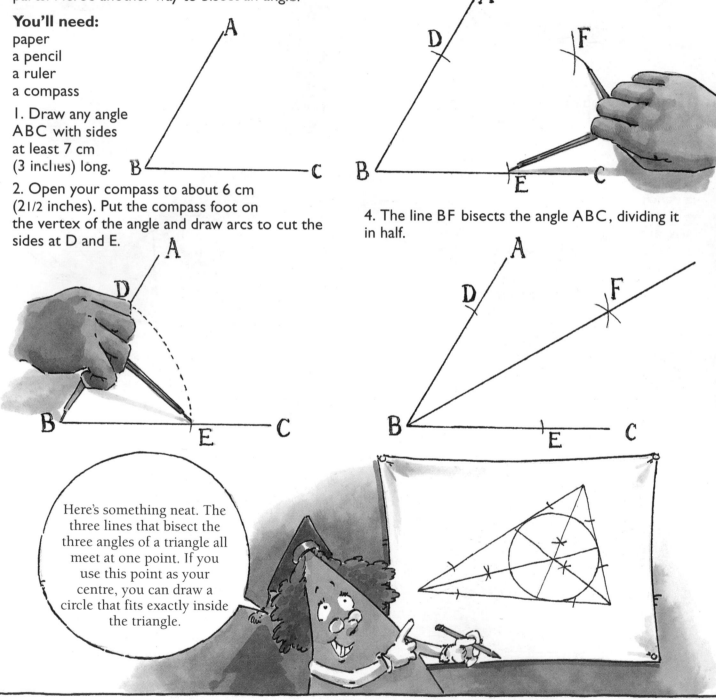

Here's something neat. The three lines that bisect the three angles of a triangle all meet at one point. If you use this point as your centre, you can draw a circle that fits exactly inside the triangle.

Area of a triangle

The ancient Egyptians got interested in geometry for a very good reason. Every year the Nile river overflowed and washed away the markers that divided one farmer's field from the next farmer's field. This meant that every year surveyors had to draw new boundaries. To make sure that each farmer got the right amount of land (and paid taxes according to the size of the field), the surveyors had to have an easy way of measuring the area of oddly shaped fields. They did it by marking off the land into big triangles and measuring the area of the triangles. They were the first to figure out how much space there is inside a triangle. Here's how to find out the area of a triangle the way the ancient Egyptians did.

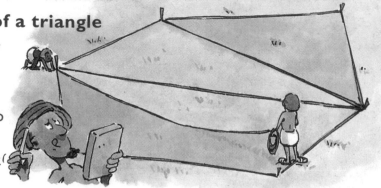

You'll need:
paper
scissors

1. Make a triangle by folding three creases in the piece of paper.

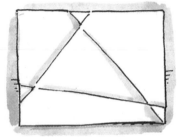

2. Cut along the creases. Label the corners of the triangle ABC.

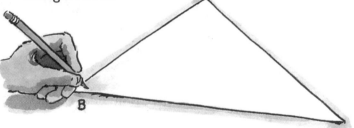

3. Fold through A so that the line BC is folded back along itself. The line you have folded is called an altitude. Label it AD.

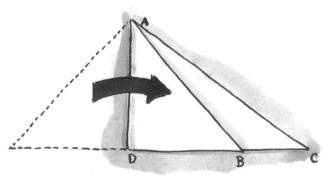

4. Fold the triangle again so that A touches D.

5. Open the triangle up. Cut off the two small triangles at the top of the original triangle as shown.

6. Rearrange the three parts to form this rectangle.

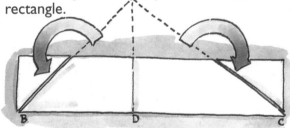

The original triangle has the same area as a rectangle having the same width but only half the height. So the area of a triangle is 1/2 times the triangle's perpendicular height (or altitude) times its base. For example, if our original triangle had a base of 4 units and an altitude of 6 units, its area would be 12 square units.

Triangular numbers

This may look like a set-up for ten-pin bowling, but it's the beginning of a pencil-and-paper game that you can play with a friend. Before you begin, you will need to figure out the trick of the triangular numbers pattern.

You'll need:
paper
a pencil

Getting ready
Set up the game board by drawing dots arranged in a triangle—one dot in the first row, two dots in the second row, five dots in the fifth row, ten dots in the tenth row and so on, for as many rows as you like. Of course, the more dots you use, the longer the game will take to finish.

Playing rules
1. Each player takes a turn drawing a line that connects two dots.

2. The point of the game is to draw a line that encloses a triangle. When you enclose a triangle, put your initial inside it.

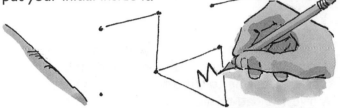

3. When the last two dots are connected, count up the triangles with your initials. The player with the most triangles wins.

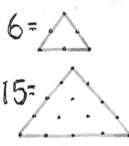

> You get an extra point for every large triangle that is made up entirely of smaller triangles initialled by you.

No matter how many rows of dots you draw, the total number of dots will be a triangular number. Triangular numbers are ones that can be arranged as shown to form triangles: 1, 3, 6, 10, 15, 21 and so on. What do you think the next triangular number will be? There is a pattern to triangular numbers. The numbers go up by adding 1, 2, 3, 4, 5 and so on to the previous number. So to get the second triangular number, you add 2 to the first number. To get the third number, you add 3 to the second number and so on. To get the seventh number, you add 7 to the sixth number. That is, you add 7 to 21 to get 28.

Pascal's triangle

You can find triangular numbers, and a lot more, in this arrangement of numbers known as Pascal's triangle. Blaise Pascal was a brilliant French mathematician who lived in the 17th century. When he was only 13, he discovered this triangle, with its very special pattern of numbers. Each number in Pascal's triangle is the sum of the two numbers immediately above it, to the left and right. Can you figure out what the next row of numbers will be? (See page 64 for the answer.)

```
              1
           1     1
         1    2    1
       1    3    3    1
      1   4    6   4    1
    1   5   10   10   5   1
   1   6  15   20  15   6   1
  1   7  21  35  35  21  7  1
```

The diagonal column 1, 3, 6, 10, 15, 21 is the series of triangular numbers.

TURN THE TRIANGLE AROUND

What is the smallest number of pennies that you have to move to change triangle A into triangle B? (See page 64 for the answer.)

A

B

Phantom triangles

Impossible tri-bar

The 20th-century mathematician Roger Penrose was the first person to draw this tricky triangle on paper, but no one can make a real one in three-dimensional space. Try it with three pencils. Each angle in this triangle looks like a normal right angle, or 90° angle. But three 90° angles add up to 270°—too many degrees to form a triangle (see page 11).

Ghostly triangles

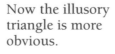

Three dots are enough to give a faint image of a second triangle, covering the gaps of the first one.

Now the illusory triangle is more obvious.

When smaller angles are cut from the circles, the triangle seems to have curved-in sides to account for the gaps.

The Bermuda triangle

Flashes of light from the sky, compasses spinning around wildly, ghost ships, lost crews, unexplained engine failures and wrecked planes. It sounds like a mystery movie, but some people think this is what you'll find if you venture into the Bermuda triangle. This mysterious triangle is the part of the Atlantic Ocean enclosed by lines joining the tips of Florida, Bermuda and Puerto Rico. Some people claim that an unknown force in this triangular area strikes down ships and airplanes and sinks them without a trace. However, many people believe that the accidents are all caused by bad weather and human error.

Triangle take-away

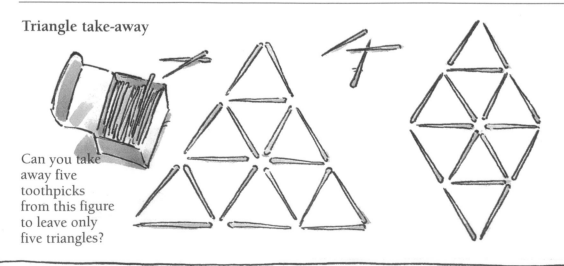

Can you take away five toothpicks from this figure to leave only five triangles?

Can you take away four toothpicks to leave only four triangles? (See page 64 for the answers.)

2 Special Triangles

Ask a friend to draw a triangle. Chances are your friend won't draw just any triangle but one of these three special models: the right triangle, the isosceles triangle or the equilateral triangle. Read on to find out why these three are old favourites.

Right triangles

Start with a square of paper, fold it in half along the diagonal, and you get a right-angled triangle. This triangle is one of the most important of all. It helped the Egyptians build the base of their pyramids and it is the shape for sails that move sailboats across the waves. It's even useful for measuring the height of tall trees or buildings. What makes this triangle special is the right angle that gives the triangle its name. A square corner, such as the corner of this book, is a right angle.

Ancient geometry

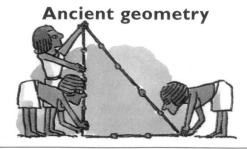

Egyptians didn't have fancy drafting tools, but they were able to make perfect right angles every time for the bases of their pyramids. The Egyptians used ropes with knots tied at equal intervals to make their measurements. It took three rope-stretchers to make the angle. Check this out for yourself. You can use black marks instead of knots if you like.

You'll need:
a piece of string about 1 metre (1 yard) long
a measuring stick
a black marker
scissors
a friend

1. Ask someone to hold the string tight along the measuring stick. Starting at one end of the string, make marks with your black marker every 4 cm (2 inches) along the string until you have made 12 equally spaced marks. Cut the string on the twelfth mark. The remaining 11 marks divide the string into 12 equal units.

2. Ask your rope-stretcher to hold together the two ends of the string. Call this point A.

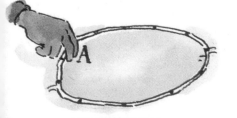

3. Count along the string until you find a mark 3 units away from A. Hold this part of the string in one hand and tighten it to make one side of the triangle.

4. Count along the string 5 more units. Hold this part of the string in your other hand.

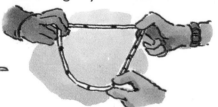

5. Pull the triangle tight. You should now have a triangle with sides three, four and five units long — count them. Check that you really have a right angle by matching it against the corner of this book. (In a triangle, the right angle is always the one across from the longest side, which is called the hypotenuse.)

What's happening?
The ancient Greek mathematician Pythagoras showed why a triangle with sides of 3, 4 and 5 units long will always contain a right angle. It's because of the way the lengths of the sides are related to one another. Pythagoras discovered a relationship that holds true for all right triangles. In what is now known as the Pythagorean theorem, Pythagoras proved that the square formed on the hypotenuse (the side opposite the right angle) has the same area as the sum of the squares formed on the other two sides.

In this triangle with sides of 3, 4 and 5 units, the square on the hypotenuse is 5^2 or $5 \times 5 = 25$ square units. Count the squares on the other two sides to see if they add up to 25.

Measuring height

Thales, the first known Greek mathematician, travelled to Egypt and amazed the Pharaoh by figuring out the height of the Great Pyramid, which rose 147 m (481 feet) above its square base with 230-m (755-foot) long sides. How did he do it? By using similar right-angled triangles. Similar triangles have exactly the same shape, even if they're not the same size. If you photocopied a triangle using the reducing button that shrinks a picture to half its size, you would end up with similar triangles. The sides of the copied triangle would be only half as long as the sides of the original triangle, but the angles would all be the same.

To measure the height of the Great Pyramid, Thales also made a smaller model of the original. At the time of day when his own shadow was the same length as his height, he measured the Great Pyramid's shadow. Since he cast a shadow as long as his own height, Thales realized that the Pyramid's shadow at that time of day must also equal its height. So, to find the pyramid's height, all he had to do was measure the length of its shadow. The similar-triangle method is a great way to measure anything that is tricky to measure directly — such as a tree, a waterfall or a tall building.

Thales had to include in his measurement the distance from the pyramid's outside wall to the centre of the pyramid below its highest point.

Isosceles triangles

Fold a piece of notepaper in half, and cut along the diagonal as shown. Unfold the paper and you have an isosceles triangle. You know that the two sides of this triangle are the same length because you just cut them out with one cut. But you might not have noticed that the angles at the base of this triangle are also the same size. The isosceles triangle has mirror symmetry—it's exactly the same on one side of the fold line as it is on the other. So two sides and two angles are exactly the same.

The isosceles triangle is a good shape for paper airplanes, darts and arrowheads. Its mirror symmetry makes each side perfectly balanced so that it flies straight. The pointy tip makes the shape streamlined and reduces air resistance. Hunters as far back as 4000 years ago used flint arrowheads that looked like isosceles triangles. Some birds and fish have also adopted a dart shape to help them speed through air and water.

70°

70°

Paper airplane math

All proper darts are symmetrical, like isosceles triangles: every fold you make on one side of the centre fold you also have to make on the other. Put this paper airplane to a flight test: what's your record for distance travelled and time spent in the air?

You'll need:

a piece of notepaper 21.6 × 28 cm (8 1/2 × 11 inches)
a pencil
a ruler
sticky tape

1. Fold the notepaper in half with the long sides together.

2. Open up the paper. Draw some lines on the paper as shown, to tell where to fold the airplane. First draw a line 10 cm (4 inches) from the top edge of the paper.

3. Draw two lines .5 cm (1/4 inch) on either side of the centre fold.

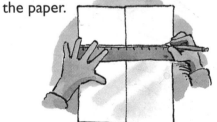

4. Make two marks at the bottom of the paper 4 cm (1 1/2 inches) from the centre fold. Starting at the top of the centre fold, draw diagonal lines to these two marks.

5. In the squares at the top of the paper, fold two right-angled triangles.

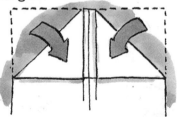

6. Fold again as shown so that the fold lines from step 5 touch the lines on either side of the middle fold.

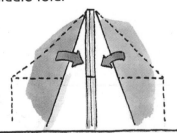

7. Fold the paper along the middle line, so the folded parts are on the outside. Sharpen the crease by running your thumbnail over the fold line and unfold.

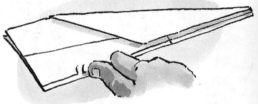

8. Now for the last step. On each side, fold along the diagonal line that you drew in step 4.

9. Hold the wings together underneath with some sticky tape. Use some sticky tape on the top to make the wings tilt slightly upwards. Now you're ready to fly.

Surveying by triangulation

Without the triangle, engineers could never have bored the Simplon tunnel through the mountains of the Alps in 1906. This tunnel connecting Switzerland and Italy is 20 km (12 miles) long. Workers started drilling from both sides of the mountain. When the two parts of the tunnel met in the middle of the mountain, they missed a perfect alignment by only 10 cm (4 inches). The surveyors had set up the drilling machines to cut along the 10-km (6-mile) sides of two very big triangles. Surveying by triangulation is based on a simple fact about a triangle. If one side and two angles of a triangle are known, the other two sides and remaining angle can be figured out easily.

You don't need to be a surveyor to use triangles for measuring distances. Every time you reach out to grab something, you use the same principle of triangulation. The triangle used here is the isosceles triangle made by your two eyes and the object your eyes are focusing on. To check this out, you'll need a friend to help out and a pen with a removable top.

1. Remove the top from the pen and hold on to the top. Give the pen to your friend. Now sit across a table from your friend and close your eyes.
2. Ask your friend to hold the pen straight up and down, about 60 cm (24 inches) in front of you.
3. Open only one eye. Try to put the top on the pen.
4. Open both eyes. How close were you? If you missed, try it again, this time with both eyes open.

What's happening?

Why do you need two eyes to figure out how far away something is? The answer lies in the triangle. If you know the length of one side — the base line — and the size of the angles on this line, you can find all three points of any triangle. In this pen experiment, you know the base line, which is the distance between your own eyes. When the muscles in your eyes contract to focus on the pen, your brain uses this information to figure out the angles on the base line. Knowing the length of the base line and the size of the two angles on the base line, your brain can calculate how far away the third point of the triangle is — the pen. But close one eye and now you know only the base line and one angle, which is not enough to reconstruct the whole triangle. Surveyors calculate distances the same way — by knowing the length of a base line and the size of the angles on the base line.

Triangle trees

Cut an isosceles triangle into a lacy tree for decorating gift boxes or hanging on your Christmas tree.

You'll need:
a square of coloured paper
scissors

1. Fold the square of paper in half diagonally.

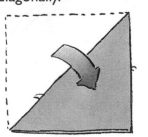

2. Fold it in half again as shown. Fold it a third time to end up with a long, narrow triangle.

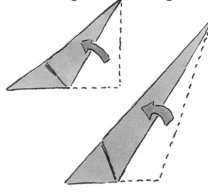

3. Trim the bottom to make the folded sides the same length. Now you have an isosceles triangle.

4. Make cuts about 1 cm (1/3 inch) apart all along one fold line. Don't cut all the way across, but leave some paper uncut at the other fold line.

5. Similarly, on the second fold line, make cuts in between the first cuts.

6. Unfold the paper. Carefully pull on the top and bottom of the triangle to open it up into a lacy, decorative triangle tree.

Equilateral triangles

The isosceles triangle has one line of symmetry (the fold line formed when you match the two equal sides together), but the equilateral triangle has three lines of symmetry. Because it has three equal sides and three equal angles, you can fold an equilateral triangle exactly in half in three different ways. An equilateral triangle is the shape of the three-leaf clover, the trillium or the iris, which also all have three lines of symmetry. In many different civilizations, people have made designs like those you see here, based on the three-fold symmetry of the equilateral triangle.

Spiral of life — ancient Irish symbol

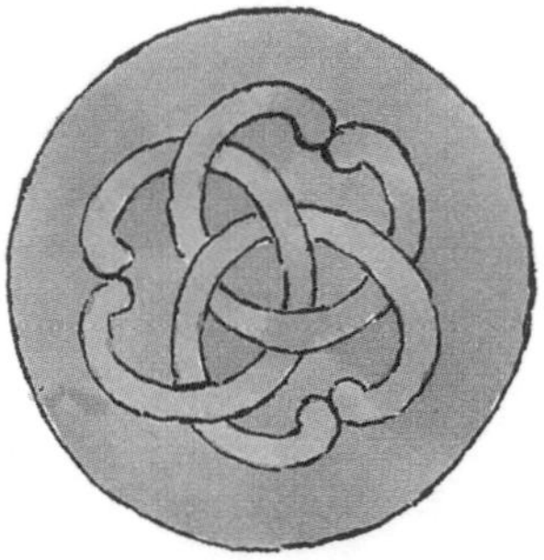

Traditional Japanese design

Modern symbol for wool products

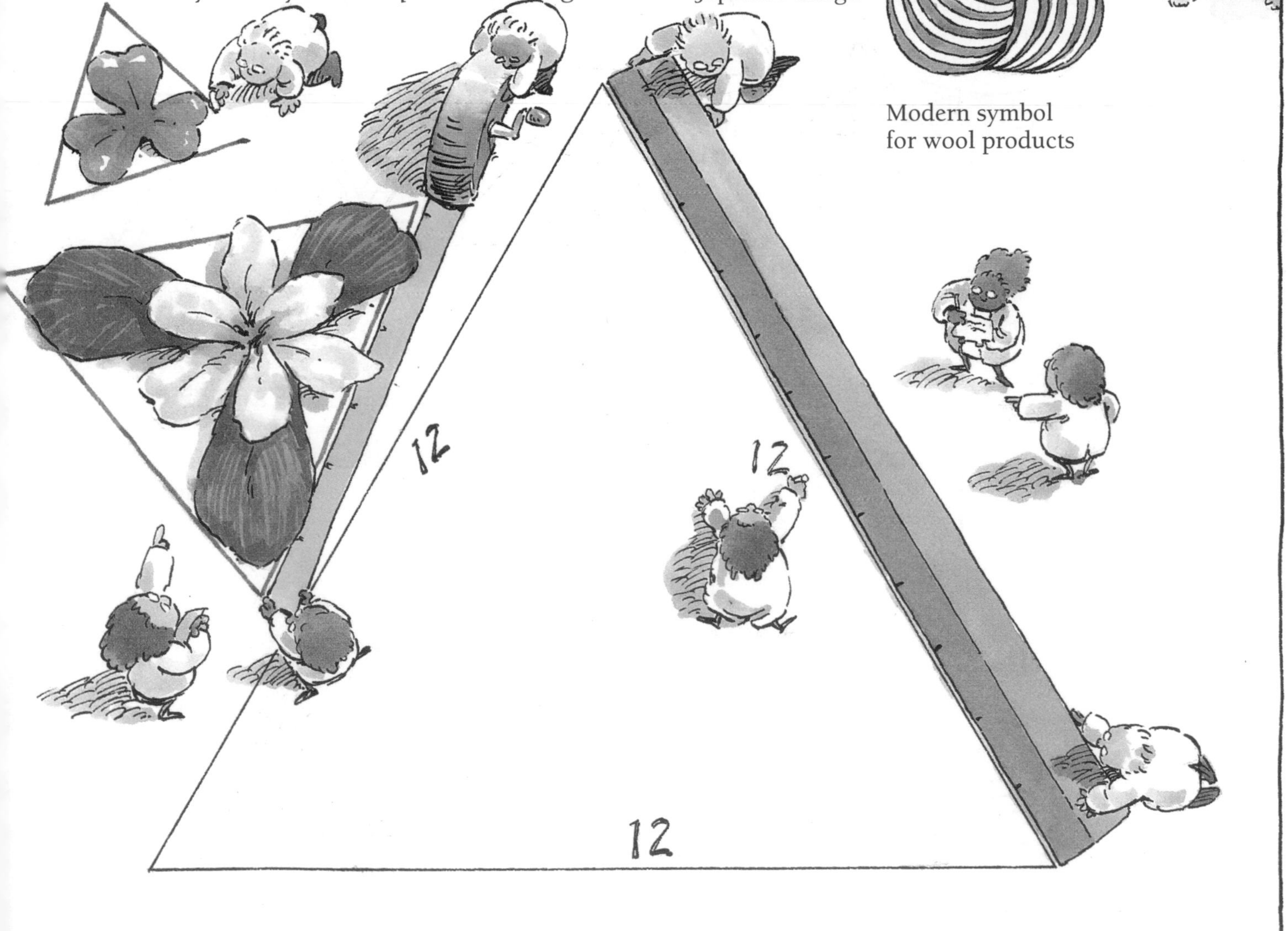

12

12

12

Equilateral designs

Starting with an equilateral triangle, you can cut out some intricate designs and see three-fold symmetry at work.

You'll need:

a square of paper

a plastic triangle used for drafting
(If you don't have a drafter's triangle, see "Fold an equilateral triangle" on page 27.)

scissors

a pencil

Use this vertex to draw the 60° angle.

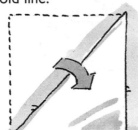

1. Fold the square in half along the diagonal. Sharpen the crease by running your thumbnail over the fold line.

2. Find the centre of the fold line by folding it in half. Mark the midpoint with a dot.

3. Line up the short side of the plastic triangle along the fold line, with the 60° vertex on the dot. Draw a line as shown. Fold along the line and sharpen the crease.

4. Fold the other side over. Sharpen the crease line.

5. Turn the paper over. Cut off the uneven edges to get an equilateral triangle.

6. Unfold the paper — you should have a hexagon, made from six equilateral triangles.

7. To get a fancier design, fold the paper back into the triangle of step 5.

8. Use your pencil to outline a design. Here are some shapes to try, or you can invent your own.

9. Unfold the paper. Because of the way you folded the paper, all your patterns will have a single design element that is repeated six times — three times as your original design, and three times as the mirror image of your design.

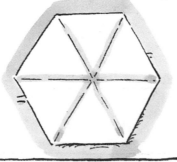

FOLD AN EQUILATERAL TRIANGLE

If you don't have a plastic triangle handy for measuring the 60° angle needed for the equilateral triangle designs, it's no problem. This folding trick gives you an equilateral triangle, which means you'll have three perfect 60° angles every time.

You'll need:
notepaper
a pencil

1. Label the corners of the piece of notepaper ABCD as shown.

2. Fold the paper in half, long sides together, so that AB touches CD. Unfold the paper.

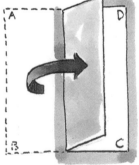

3. Fold the short side BC so that C touches the fold line.

4. With this folded side as the base, fold the right side down so that the edge of the paper is lined up along the base.

5. Fold the extra paper on the left side under as shown. Check to see that you really have an equilateral triangle. Match the angles by placing them one on top of the other. Are the angles all the same size? Are the sides all the same length?

To make a hexagon, or six-sided shape, fold in the corners of the equilateral triangle so that they meet in the centre of the triangle.

Triangle weave

The triangle spider is an expert in weaving triangular webs. But you don't need to be a triangle spider to weave this amazing design. Start with an equilateral triangle, and turn some straight lines into curves.

You'll need:

a square of stiff cardboard with sides at least 22 cm (9 inches) long (Cardboard must be stiff or it won't lie flat when the threads are woven.)
a ruler
a plastic triangle or a compass
a pencil
scissors
3 colours of thread, each about 2.7 m (3 yards) long. Use contrasting colours that will show up well against the cardboard.

Draw an equilateral triangle

1. Near the bottom of the square of cardboard, draw a line 20 cm (8 inches) long, parallel to the edge. This line will be the base of an equilateral triangle.

2. Use the plastic triangle to construct a 60° angle at one end of the base line. (If you don't have a plastic triangle handy, use your compass to construct a small equilateral triangle at one end of the base. See "Dissection puzzle" on page 30 to find out how.)

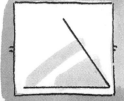

3. Extend the second line to make it 20 cm (8 inches) long.

4. Draw the third side. Check with your ruler to make sure that this third side is also 20 cm (8 inches) long.

Prepare the triangle for weaving

5. Use a ruler and pencil to mark the sides every 1 cm (1/2 inch). You should have 19 marks on each side (15 if you are using inches).

6. Cut out the triangle.

7. At each mark, make a short cut at right angles to the sides of the triangle. Then make a short cut at each of the three vertexes. These cuts are the slots that will hold the thread when you are weaving.

Weave some curves

8. This is the tricky part. But numbering the slots on the back of the cardboard will help you put the threads in the right place. Start at a vertex and number each cut along one side from 1 up to 20 (16 if you are working in inches). Number the slots on the other side of the same vertex by working back from 20 (or 16) to 1.

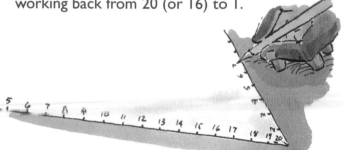

9. Cut a piece of thread that is about 2.7 m (3 yards) long. Pull the thread up through slot 1 at the vertex. Leave about 10 cm (4 inches) of thread as a tail to tie up later. Stretch the long end of the thread across the front of the triangle to slot 1 on the other side. On the back, stretch the thread to slot 2 and pull it through.

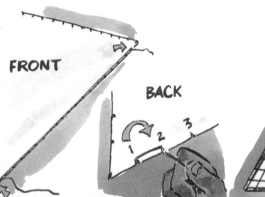

10. On the front, stretch the thread to the opposite side to slot 2. Keep weaving the thread from side to side as shown. If you are putting the thread in the right slots, the back of the triangle will look like this. When you get to the last slot and have completed the curve, pull the thread to the back and tie it to the other end of the thread.

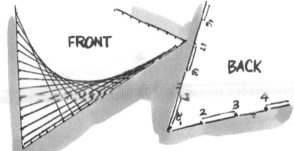

11. Weave the other two curves in the same way.

REULEAUX TRIANGLE

At the centre of your triangle weave, you will see an interesting shape, called a Reuleaux triangle, which is far more useful than it looks. What makes it special is that, like a circle, the Reuleaux triangle is a curve of constant width. The Philadelphia Fire Department has used this shape since the 1950s for the fire hydrant shaft that controls the water. This way they keep their fire hydrants safe from pranksters who want to chill out in the summer heat. Viewed from the top, the fire hydrant shaft looks like an equilateral triangle with curved sides. Since the Reuleaux triangle is a curve of constant width, the parallel jaws of an ordinary wrench slip around and around it, the way they would around a circle. This makes it difficult, or impossible for most people to turn them. (Fire fighters carry their own specially shaped wrenches to turn on the water.)

Dissection puzzle

This dissection puzzle is like Humpty Dumpty—a lot easier to take apart than it is to put together again. Once you've made the puzzle, challenge a friend to put it together.

You'll need:

Bristol board or cardboard (it's best to use something that is the same colour on both sides—it makes the puzzles trickier to solve)
a pencil
a ruler
a compass
scissors
paper

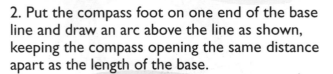

1. You're going to draw an equilateral triangle on the Bristol board. Start by drawing the base. A base of 7 cm (3 inches) works well.

2. Put the compass foot on one end of the base line and draw an arc above the line as shown, keeping the compass opening the same distance apart as the length of the base.

3. Put the compass foot on the other end of the line and draw a second arc to intersect the first arc. This intersection point is the third vertex of the triangle. Draw the other two sides of the triangle.

4. Cut out the triangle.

5. Before you cut out the puzzle, draw a diagram of the cuts you plan to make. Here are some examples of some four-piece puzzles and some six-piece puzzles, but let your imagination go wild and design your own.

6. Cut out the puzzle. The puzzle you designed may be so tricky that even you can't put the pieces back together! But you can always consult your diagram if you're stumped.

Triangle fractals

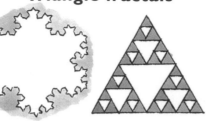

Mathematicians call these strange shapes "fractals." Each part of the design is a miniature of the whole design. You can find fractals in nature if you look carefully at a cross-section of broccoli or cauliflower. See how each small part is a tiny version of the whole thing. An ordinary equilateral triangle is the starting point for both of the fractals shown here.

You'll need:
white paper
a pencil
a ruler
a compass
a black marker

The Sierpinski gasket

A Sierpinski gasket is a fractal formed by taking away the small triangle formed when you bisect the sides of an equilateral triangle and connect the midpoints.

1. Draw an equilateral triangle.

2. Bisect the sides.

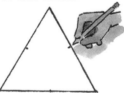

3. Draw lines connecting the midpoints of the sides to form four smaller triangles.

4. Leave the middle triangle alone. Repeat steps 2 and 3 with the other three triangles.

5. Repeat as many times as you like, each time leaving the middle triangle alone.

6. Leave the middle triangles white, and colour the others black, as shown. Each time you remove small triangles from the centre, you have less and less black space in the design. Eventually you would end up with all white space.

Koch snowflake

For this fractal you don't take away triangles; you add them. You make a Koch snowflake by adding small equilateral triangles to the sides of larger triangles. After a few steps, you get a lacy snowflake.

1. Draw an equilateral triangle with sides of 12 cm (6 inches).

2. Measure the sides and divide them exactly into three equal sections.

3. Make a smaller equilateral triangle on the middle section of the sides.

4. Continue as before. Divide the sides of the smaller triangles in three and construct a smaller equilateral triangle on the middle section of the sides.

5. Repeat as many times as you like. With each step, you make the perimeter around the outside of the triangle longer.

This shape was named after Helge von Koch, who first discovered it in 1904 when he was studying curves.

Hexaflexagon

Transform a chain of equilateral triangles into a puzzle that flips and twists and turns itself inside out.

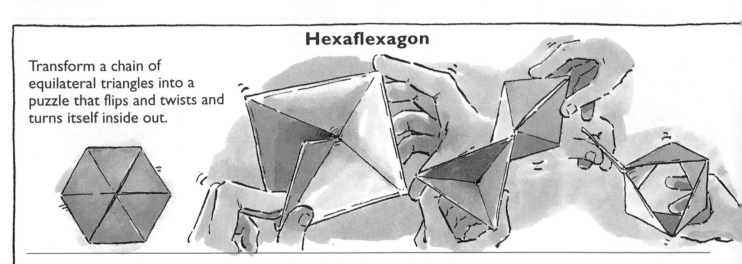

You'll need:

yellow or white Bristol board
a pencil
a ruler
a plastic triangle with a 60° angle
scissors
glue
two contrasting colours of poster paint and a paintbrush

1. Measure and cut a strip of Bristol board that is about 5 cm by 35 cm (2 inches by 14 inches). A smaller or larger strip is fine—just cut your strip seven times as long as it is wide.

2. Placing the 60° angle on the strip as shown, draw a line to the top of the strip. This line is the first side of an equilateral triangle.

3. Placing the 60° angle along this line, draw a second line to complete the triangle.

4. Draw nine more triangles the same way.

5. Trim off the ends to leave a strip of triangles.

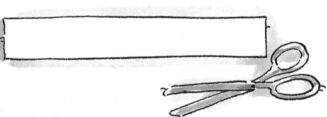

6. Use the point of the compass to score the zig-zag lines. This will make the cardboard easier to fold. Fold back and forth along each fold line.

Tetrahedron

Square pyramid

Octahedron

Before you fold and glue the strip into a hexaflexagon, experiment with making these three-dimensional shapes. Check out how many triangles meet at one vertex.

Petal shape

7. Lay out the strip as shown and number the triangles.

8. Flip the strip over and label the triangles on the back. Make sure that triangle 11 is the back of triangle 1.

9. To fold the hexaflexagon, hold the strip as shown and fold triangle 11 over triangle 12. Then fold triangle 15 on triangle 14. Fold triangle 8 on triangle 7.

A

B

C

10. Glue triangle 10 to triangle 1. (If you end up with a different arrangement, you have folded it wrong and should try again.)

11. When the glue is dry, carefully paint each side of the hexaflexagon a different colour and let dry.

12. Gently twist the hexaflexagon along the folds until it flattens into a different colour pattern. How many different patterns can you find?

What's an octopus?

An eight-sided cat.

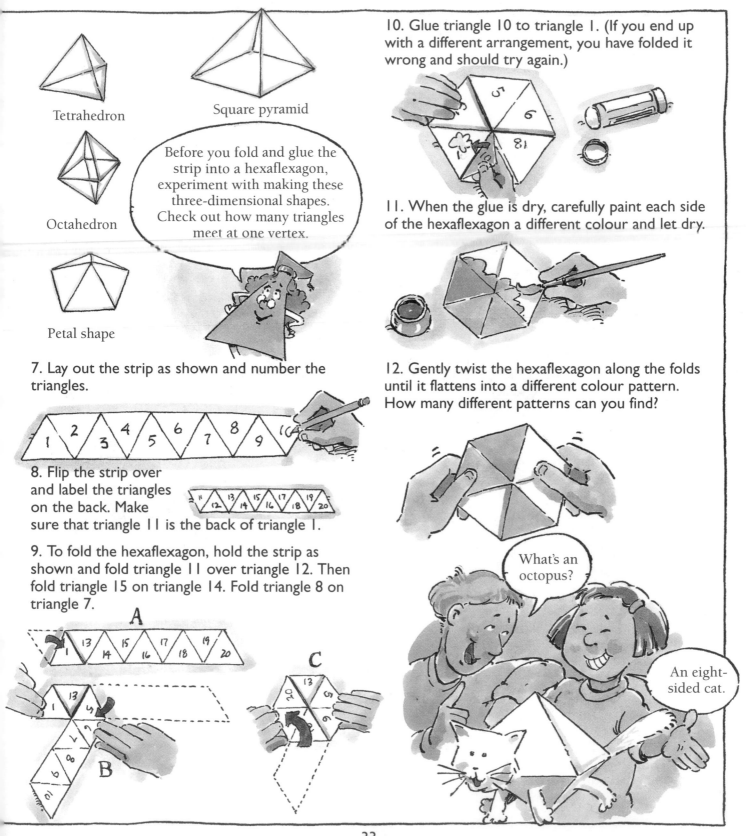

3 Building with Triangles

If you were on a moving train or ferry boat, how would you stand to keep your balance? If you stood with your legs apart, you'd be turning yourself into a human triangle. Triangles are stable and strong. That's why builders and architects use them for lightweight bridges and towers. As you have seen, you can push a square out of shape by pinching its corners together, but you can't squash a triangle. The only structure that holds its shape under pressure is a triangle.

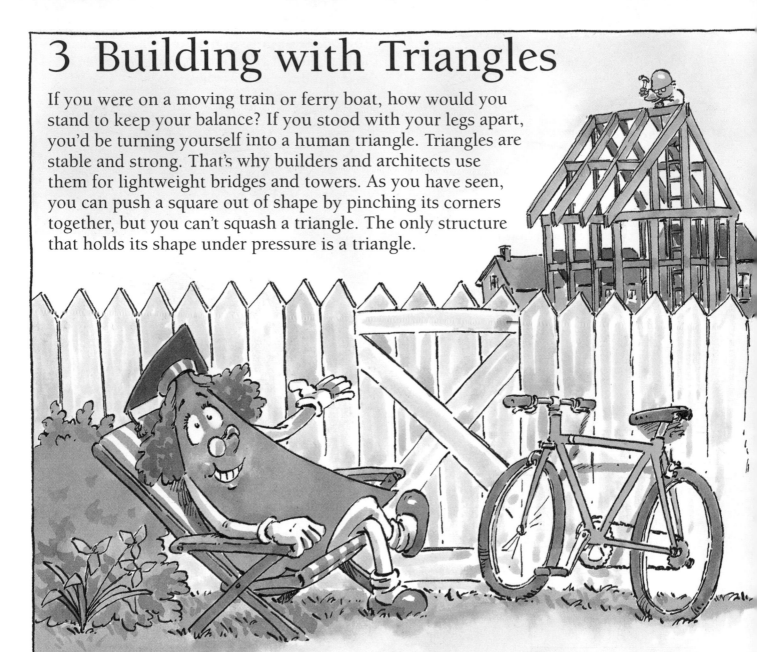

Look around you. Can you find examples of triangles that make things strong? You probably didn't think of the hidden triangle in a slice of green pepper. Since the green pepper is almost hollow inside, it's much lighter than a solid fruit of the same size, such as an orange. The green pepper keeps its firm, rounded shape because of its inner triangular ribs.

How about a shelf support, an ironing board, a window fastening holding a window open, a bicycle frame, a deck chair, a gate or the timbers in the roof? Triangles strengthen hydro towers and the cross-arms of telephone poles. The long boom of a building crane is made of relatively thin pieces of steel, but its triangular shape makes it strong enough to hoist heavy machines to the top of a high-rise building. Triangles are strong and rigid because of one key fact: a triangle can't change its shape unless one of its sides gets longer or shorter.

Putting triangles to work

Take a piece of paper and hold it at the corners along one edge. See how it droops—it can't support even its own weight. So how could you make it stronger? You could glue some cardboard stiffeners along its length. But you don't need anything that fancy—just some triangles. Try this strength test.

You'll need:
paper
2 boxes
some paperback books

1. Fold the paper into a fan.

2. Support the ends of the fan on two boxes to make a bridge structure.

3. Test the strength of your bridge by putting a paperback book on it. Keep adding books until the bridge breaks.

What's happening?
The same piece of paper that couldn't support even itself can now hold the weight of several books. You've made the original paper at least 300 times stronger by folding it into triangles. Triangles are also what makes corrugated cardboard strong enough to use for cartons for packing groceries. If you cut into a piece of corrugated cardboard, you will see an inside layer of triangular folds sandwiched between the two outer layers of paper.

Bridges

Building a bridge over a small stream is a snap. Put some planks across the stream and you're ready to go. But what if the stream is too wide for the plank to reach across? Try this bridge-building experiment, using only cardboard strips and paper fasteners. Test out different ways to connect the strips together to make a section at least 30 cm (12 inches) long.

You'll need:
Bristol board
a ruler
a pencil
scissors
a one-hole punch
a package of paper fasteners

1. Cut out 15 strips of Bristol board that are 12 cm (5 inches) long and 1 cm (1/3 inch) wide. (You can reuse the cardboard strips from "Making triangles," page 7.)

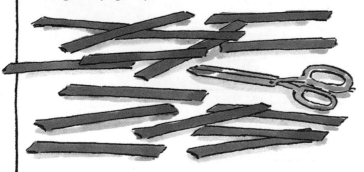

2. Punch holes at each end of the Bristol board strips.

3. Use the strips and paper fasteners to make a bridge at least 30 cm (12 inches) long.

Put your bridge to the test by using it to span two stacks of books set 20 cm (8 inches) apart.

If you used triangles to build your bridge, you get an A+ in engineering skills. As you can see, you don't need long pieces of building material to span a wide gap. Short ones will work as long as they are locked together into triangles, as they are in the famous bridges shown on the next two pages.

Railway bridges

The bridge you built from cardboard strips is actually called a truss and looks like the railway trusses built in North America more than a hundred years ago during the great age of trains. Thousands of new bridges were built to span the deep gorges and wild rivers of the continent. The problem is that the longer a bridge is, the heavier it gets. If it is very long, it can break under its own weight. A bridge builder can always reduce a bridge's weight by using less building material. But since the bridge has to be strong enough to support the extra weight of a thundering train,

the bridge builder doesn't want to reduce weight at the expense of strength or rigidity.

The solution is to cut away all the material not actually needed to give the bridge strength. When all the inessential material is cut away, you are left with open structures that are light because they are full of holes, or meshes. Strength and rigidity come from the design miracle — the triangle. This airy bridge of triangles was built in 1901 over the Dead Horse Gulch near the White Pass in British Columbia, Canada.

These patterns aren't string games; they're different trusses patented during the railway era and named after their inventors. Zigzag cross-bars connect the parallel bars on the top and bottom to form N-shapes, M-shapes or W-shapes — they all work as long as they form the chain of triangles needed for strength and rigidity.

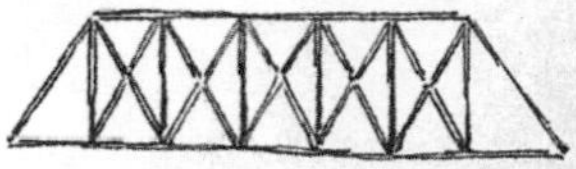

Howe truss

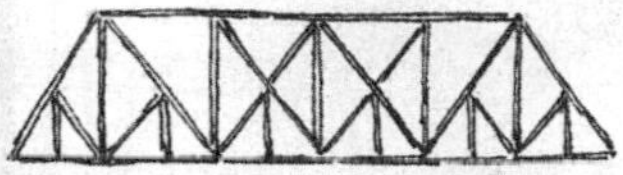

Baltimore truss

Whipple bowstring truss

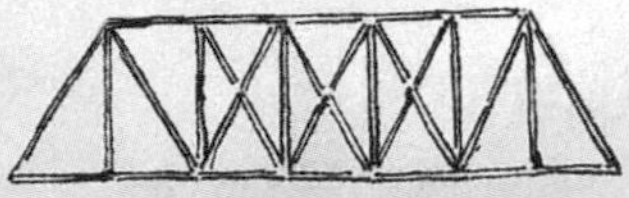

Pratt truss

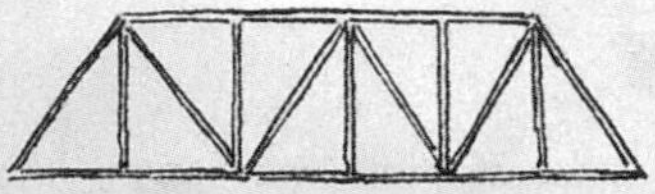

Warren truss

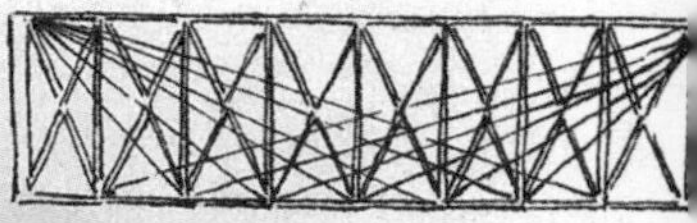

Bollman truss

The Firth of Forth Bridge in Scotland (shown here), completed in 1890 with a span of 529 m (1735 feet), is still one of the great bridges of the world.

Monuments

The Eiffel Tower

Before he designed the Eiffel Tower for the Paris exhibition of 1889, Gustave Eiffel had already built many iron viaducts and bridges and had learned a lot about using triangulated structures to resist the blows of wind and water. Nevertheless, for his tower, he didn't leave anything to chance. Before starting the building, he made over 5000 drawings of all parts of the tower, drawings that called for 15 000 structural pieces and 2 500 000 rivet holes.

At 300 m (986 feet), his wrought-iron tower rose almost twice as high as the 1884 Washington Monument, till then the world's tallest structure. The Eiffel Tower weighs about 6350 t (7000 tons) — if you think that sounds heavy, compare it to the Washington Monument's 89 000 t (81 000 tons) of stone. The Washington Monument gets its strength from the sheer weight of its piled stone, but the Eiffel Tower is strong through good design. Like the truss, the Eiffel Tower is mostly air and a lacy frame of triangles. If you melted its frame down, it would form a block about 5 cm (2 inches) thick that would fit under its own four legs.

Although in the beginning some people complained that the Eiffel Tower "stood up from Paris like a hatpin," now it's the most famous building in France.

Giant egg

To celebrate the 100th anniversary of the Royal Canadian Mounted Police in 1974, the Alberta government offered grants for community projects. A giant statue of a Mountie, a Maple Leaf or some other standard Canadian symbol was not good enough for the town of Vegreville, Alberta. Vegreville proposed to build a 3 1/2-storey-high Ukrainian Easter Egg, or Pysanka, to honour the Ukrainian pioneers who had settled the area.

Who could they get to build an egg 10 m (31 feet) high? Finally Ronald Resch, a computer science professor from the University of Utah, took on the job. For the movie *Star Trek*, he had designed the techno-mouth of a spaceship that swallowed up everything in its path. Resch's plan for the egg was to make it using many flat tiles joined together at slight angles.

So what shape should the tiles be? It's cheaper to produce tiles if they can all be made the same shape. There are only three regular shapes that will cover a flat surface without overlapping or leaving gaps — the square, the hexagon and the equilateral triangle. Resch discovered that he could tile the egg with 1108 same-sized, equilateral triangles if he interspersed them with 524 three-pointed stars.

How well has this egg survived wind, water and gravity? After all, Humpty Dumpty had problems. "We've had no trouble with the Pysanka in any way," said Vegreville's mayor. "The structure was made to last." The egg sits serenely on its base of concrete and steel and turns in the wind like a weather-vane.

Buildings

Did you know that triangles brace high-rise buildings against the wind so that people on the top floor don't get dizzy? In some steel skyscrapers, the elevator shaft at the centre is surrounded by a cage made of four triangulated frames that run all the way from the bottom right up to the top of the building. These Xed-frames are actually trusses, with the same qualities of lightness and strength.

Usually the Xed-frame is hidden at the building's core, but in the John Hancock Insurance Company Building in Chicago the frame of triangles was put on the outside. Smart real estate agents charge more rent to the two offices on each floor that have a window blocked by the diagonal frame — they say it's a status symbol.

Sydney Opera House

The Danish architect Jøern Utzon never really expected to win the 1957 competition to design the Sydney Opera House in Australia. In fact, when people first looked at his design, they said it was weird and not very useful. His plans called for a series of ten concrete vaults, like big triangular sails, up to 60 m (200 feet) high, rising one behind the other. Utzon came up with the triangular shapes for his vaults by slicing different segments out of three wooden balls. The building was opened as a performing arts centre in 1973 and has become a famous landmark. Rising above Sydney Harbour, it suggests water, waves and sails.

Roofs

Triangles are a clue to weather and climate. To see how, fold a piece of paper in half and set it on the table as shown. Quebec farmhouses and Swiss chalets need roofs this steep so that the snow will slide off. Open up the sides of the paper a bit, and you get a gentle slope suited to climates with rain but not much snow. Flatten the paper right out, and you get a roof suitable for Mexico or the Mediterranean, where it is hot and dry. From this map showing roof slopes, you can figure out which places are cold and snowy, which places have rain but not much snow, which places are hot with lots of rain and which places are dry and hot.

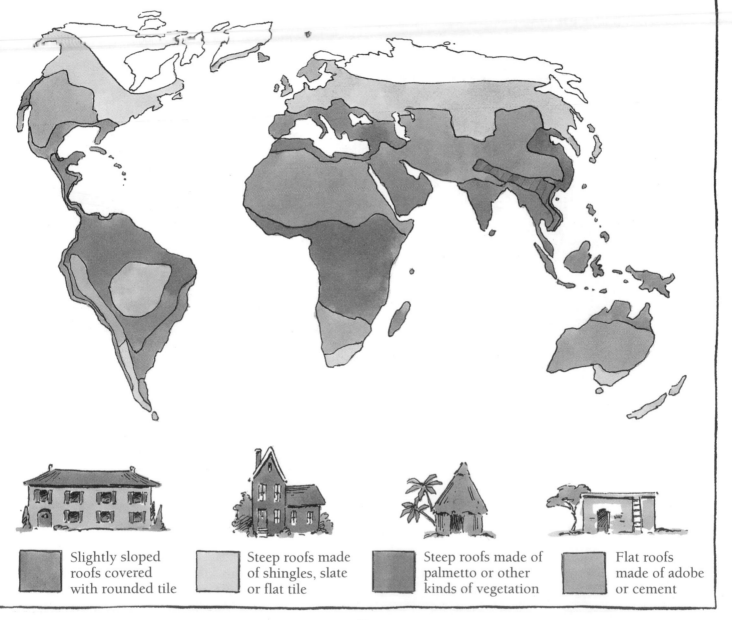

- Slightly sloped roofs covered with rounded tile
- Steep roofs made of shingles, slate or flat tile
- Steep roofs made of palmetto or other kinds of vegetation
- Flat roofs made of adobe or cement

4 Triangular Prism

When you think of a prism, you may think of a piece of glass that breaks up the sunlight into rainbow colours. But the word "prism" really refers to a shape. A prism is a solid figure. A prism must have a base and a top that are parallel and the same size and shape, and the sides of a prism must be parallelograms. The secret to identifying a prism is counting the number of sides in the prism's base — three sides make a triangular prism, four sides make a rectangular prism, five sides make a pentagonal prism, six sides make a hexagonal prism (the shape bees use for the cells in their honeycombs) and 20 sides make a 20-sided prism.

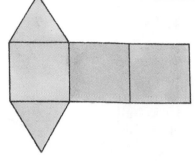

Mathematicians call this a net for making a triangular prism. It uses an equilateral triangle, so the rectangular sides are all the same width. But you can make a prism from any kind of triangle, including scalene triangles.

A parallelogram is a four-sided shape with opposite sides that are parallel.

If you set a triangular prism down on one of its rectangular faces, you have a shape like an A-frame house, which does a great job of keeping snow off the roof. If you flatten out the triangular face, you get a wedge shape, which is the shape of an axe.

If oranges could be grown in the shape of triangular prisms, fruit growers could pack them together to fill up all the space in the crate, without leaving any gaps or air-holes in between.

Make your own kaleidoscope

The kaleidoscope was invented around 1816, and it's been a hit ever since. With this prism-shaped toy, you can produce new symmetrical designs with a flick of the wrist.

You'll need:

3 small mirrors (not round ones) that are all the same size (you can get them in a drugstore)

masking tape

a pencil

a small piece of stiff, clear plastic (e.g., the kind you find as baked goods covers in grocery stores)

scissors

a small piece of waxed paper

paper of different colours

1. Tape the three purse mirrors together as shown to form the sides of a triangular prism.

Before you go further, discover how reflections in the three mirrors work to create patterns. Draw a large comma shape like this on a piece of paper. Put the prism over top of the paper so that the comma shape is near one of the vertexes. How many reflections do you get? Are all the reflections the same?

2. Trace the base of the triangular prism on the clear plastic sheet, and cut out the triangle. Repeat this step to get a second clear plastic triangle.

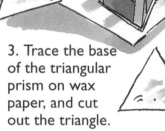

3. Trace the base of the triangular prism on wax paper, and cut out the triangle.

4. Cut the coloured paper into small confetti-sized pieces.

5. Put tape along the edges of one plastic triangle so that half the tape sticks out as shown.

6. Make a sandwich of triangles. Start with the taped plastic triangle (make sure the sticky side is facing up). Cover the triangle with the piece of wax paper. Add the small pieces of coloured paper. Cover with the second plastic triangle.

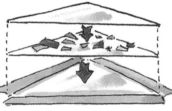

7. Put the prism over the triangle sandwich and secure the tape.

8. Hold the kaleidoscope up to your eye and look towards a light source (but don't look directly into the sun). The pattern of coloured paper is reflected six times to make an intricate design. Shake the kaleidoscope each time you want another pattern.

Make a construction kit

With this construction kit, you can make prisms and lots more shapes too. If you have enough construction units, you can make octet trusses, twisty shapes and even wheels. Just make sure that the sides of the construction units are all the same length so that the squares and triangles fit together.

You'll need:
Bristol board or cardboard
a pencil
a ruler
a compass
scissors
a one-hole punch
a box of 5-cm (2-inch) elastics

1. Draw an equilateral triangle with sides 10 cm (4 inches) long (see "Dissection puzzle" on page 30 for instructions). Use the pointed end of the compass to score the lines outlining the triangle.

2. Draw a slightly larger triangle as a .5 cm (1/4 inch) frame around the first one. Cut out the larger triangle.

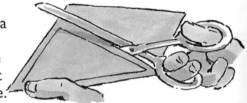

3. Punch a hole at each vertex of the small triangle. Trim the corners and fold up the edges along the score lines.

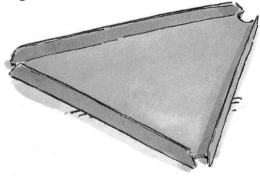

4. You need at least one additional triangle for the prism. Make more triangular units the same way. (With 20 triangles, you can go wild and make an icosohedron.)

5. Now make a square unit. Draw a square with sides 10 cm (4 inches) long. Use the pointed end of the compass to score the lines outlining the square.

6. Draw a slightly larger square as a .5 cm (1/4 inch) frame around the first one. Cut out the larger square.

7. Punch a hole at each corner of the small square. Trim the corners and fold up the edges along the score lines.

8. You need at least two more square units for the prism. Make more square units the same way.

9. To make a prism, start by lining up two squares as shown to form an edge. Join them by fitting an elastic over the punched holes.

10. Use two more elastics to attach the third square. This gives you the three sides of the triangular prism.

11. With three elastics, attach one triangle to form a top.

12. With three more elastics, attach the second triangle to form a base and complete the prism.

13. When you are finished with your construction, remove the elastics and recycle the building units for other structures. Store the building units in a big plastic ice cream container.

The equilateral triangle and the square are both regular polygons. In a regular polygon, all the sides are the same length and all the angles are equal.

Platonic solids

You can use your construction kit from page 44 to make some neat shapes called Platonic solids. Sound like something from outer space? Well, the Platonic solids are simply shapes, but they all have two things in common. First they have faces that are congruent, regular polygons. This means that each face in a Platonic solid has equal angles as well as sides that are the same length (like the square and the equilateral triangle you just made), and each face is the same size and shape. Second, the same number of faces must meet at each vertex. The Platonic solids are the only five shapes possible that meet these requirements, and you can make four of them with your construction kit.

Icosohedron
Use 20 equilateral triangles. Fit five triangles around each vertex.

Tetrahedron
Use four equilateral triangles. Fit three triangles around each vertex.

Cube
Use six square units. Fit three around each vertex.

Octahedron
Use eight equilateral triangles. Fit four triangles around each vertex.

Dodecahedron
To make the fifth Platonic solid, you need regular pentagons, which have five sides all the same length. Use 12 pentagonal units. Fit three pentagons around each vertex.

IT MUST BE A SIGN

Triangles can mean many things, depending on who is reading the signs. Here are some of the meanings that triangles have for different people:

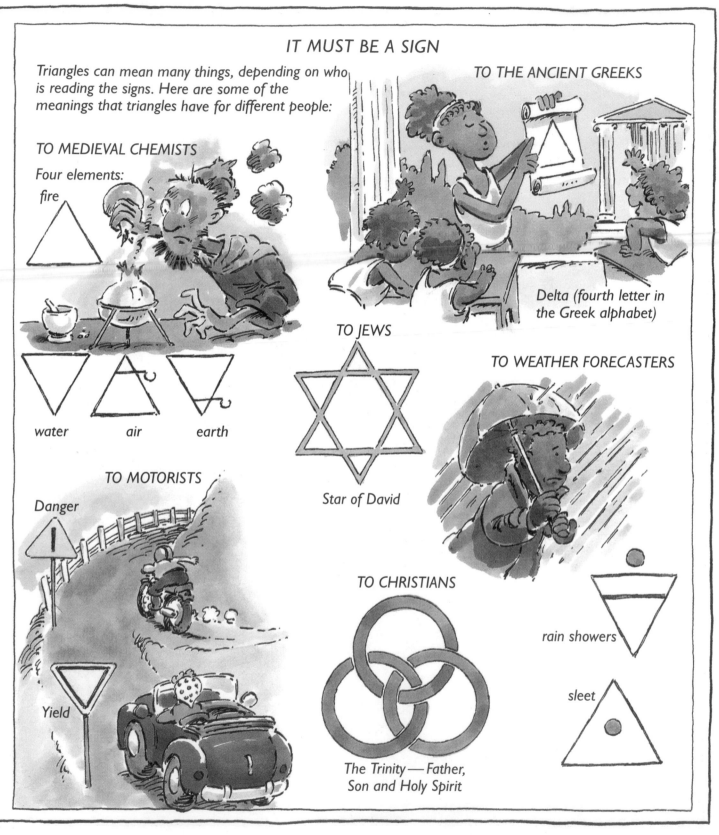

TO MEDIEVAL CHEMISTS

Four elements:

fire

water   air   earth

TO THE ANCIENT GREEKS

Delta (fourth letter in the Greek alphabet)

TO JEWS

Star of David

TO MOTORISTS

Danger

Yield

TO CHRISTIANS

The Trinity — Father, Son and Holy Spirit

TO WEATHER FORECASTERS

rain showers

sleet

Newton's prism

Have you ever wondered about the mini-rainbow that you see when light shines through an aquarium or a piece of glass? Why does this happen? The great scientist Isaac Newton wondered about this too, and in 1665 he began experimenting with light, lenses and prisms. He was intrigued by the fact that when sunlight passes through a glass prism, the light comes out in separate coloured bands. In one experiment, he arranged the shutters on his window to allow only a narrow beam of sunlight into the room. Then he held a prism in this light beam. He saw that the light passing through the prism fell onto the far wall in the colours of the rainbow — red, orange, yellow, green, blue, indigo and violet.

With more experimenting, he discovered that light travelling through a prism fans out into separate bands of colour because the prism bends some of the light more than it bends others. Red light travels fastest and is bent the least in passing through the prism. Violet light travels slowest and is bent the most. That's why the red band is always on the top and the violet band is always on the bottom of a rainbow, with the other colours ranged in between. During a shower, falling water droplets act like little prisms to split light into its colours to make a rainbow. If you want to try Newton's experiment, you can buy a prism in a science store, or you can make your own light-catcher by growing an alum crystal.

Grow an alum crystal

An alum crystal has the shape of an octahedron. Hang your crystal in a window, and its eight triangular faces will catch the sun to make mini-rainbows.

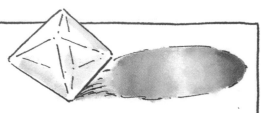

You'll need:

an adult helper
water
a measuring cup
alum (short for aluminum potassium sulfate; found in drug stores or in the spice section of grocery stores)
measuring spoon
a bowl
white thread
a paper coffee filter (or several layers of paper towel)
a glass jar
a pencil
cardboard

1. Have an adult pour 60 mL (1/4 cup) of boiling water into the measuring cup.

2. Add 30 mL (2 tbsp) alum to the water and stir to dissolve the alum in the water. There will be a few grains of alum at the bottom of the cup that won't dissolve.

3. Pour the alum solution into the bowl and set it aside for a few days on a shelf where it won't be disturbed.

4. When crystals have formed in the bottom of the bowl, pour off the alum solution. Examine the crystals. Pick out the one that is biggest and best formed to use as a seed crystal. A well-shaped crystal will have triangular faces.

5. Cut a length of white thread about as long as your forearm. Tie one end carefully around the seed crystal and set the crystal aside until you have finished steps 6 to 8.

6. Put 60 mL (4 tbsp) of alum into a measuring cup.

7. Have an adult add small amounts of boiling water gradually to the cup containing the alum. (You need boiling water because more alum dissolves in hot water than in water at room temperature.) Between each new addition of water, stir well to dissolve the alum. Keep adding water gradually until almost all the alum has dissolved.

8. Let the solution cool. (If you put your seed crystal into a hot solution, the crystal might dissolve instead of grow.)

9. Pour the cooled solution through the coffee filter into the glass jar to strain out any remaining undissolved alum crystals.

10. Wrap and tie the thread around a pencil as shown. Use the pencil to hang the crystal in the alum solution in the glass jar. The crystal should be in the middle of the solution, not too close to the walls of the jar.

11. Cover the jar with a piece of cardboard and set it on a shelf for two weeks or more. Watch the crystal grow.

5 Tetrahedron

Can you use only six toothpicks to make four equilateral triangles? Give up? No matter how many ways you arrange the toothpicks on a flat table, you can't solve this puzzle in two dimensions. But if you work in three dimensions, the problem is easy. Here's how. With three toothpicks, form a flat triangle on the table, using little balls of Plasticine to hold the corners together. Use the other three toothpicks to make a fourth vertex in the air as shown. With your six toothpicks, you have made four equilateral triangles. The four triangles are the sides, or faces, of a tetrahedron.

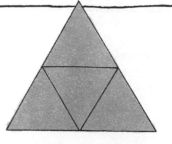

This net can be used for constructing a tetrahedron. You can make a larger net by tracing around a cardboard equilateral triangle four times to produce this arrangement of four triangles. Then cut out and fold along the lines.

Another way to visualize a tetrahedron is to stack four oranges together. If you could draw lines joining the centres of the four oranges, you would have a tetrahedron.

As you might guess, the tetrahedron is a very strong and stable shape. This is because each of its triangular sides is so strong. The tetrahedron is the polyhedron (many-sided solid shape) with the fewest possible sides. It also has the least possible volume, or space inside it, in relation to its outside surface. This large surface area makes the tetrahedron a good shape for a space satellite. One of the world's tiniest satellites is a tetrahedron with sides of 13 cm (5 inches). No matter how it tumbles around in space it will always have one or more sides towards the sun to absorb energy and one or more sides away from the sun for cooling.

Make a tetrahedral gift box

Here's a great way to put tetrahedra to work—make a tetrahedral gift box.

You'll need:
paper (any size and colour, even a big piece of newspaper)
a pencil
a compass
scissors
sticky tape

1. Draw the largest circle your compass will make— this will make a gift box large enough to hold something the size of a golf ball. Mark the centre of the circle with a dot. Cut out the circle. (If you want a gift box big enough to hold something the size of a grapefruit, use a dinner plate to draw the circle. Cut out the circle and fold in half twice to find the circle's centre at the intersection of the two fold lines.)

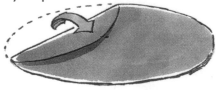

2. To get the first side of a triangle, fold any point on the outside, or circumference, of the circle so that the point touches the centre of the circle where you put the dot.

3. Make a second fold as shown, so that the second fold starts at one end of the first fold line and the circumference touches the dot.

4. Make the third side of the triangle by folding the remaining circumference to touch the dot. (If your triangle doesn't have three sharp, well-formed angles, you should unfold it and start again.)

5. Fold one of the sides in half to find its midpoint. Fold the opposite vertex down to touch this midpoint. Sharpen the fold line by running your thumbnail over it. You now have a small triangle in between two others.

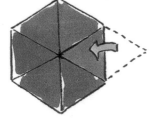

6. Fold the outside triangles on top of the inside triangle. Crease the fold lines.

7. To form a tetrahedron, join the vertexes of the original large triangle as shown. Put your present inside, tape the sides shut, and add a celebration bow, if you like.

As a gift-box variation for a flat present, make a cut-off, or truncated, tetrahedron. There are just a few more steps:

8. Skip step 7. After step 6, unfold to get the original large triangle. Fold the vertices in to touch the dot at the centre of the circle. Crease the fold lines. You now have a hexagon.

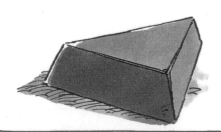

9. Fold the sides up and interlock to make this flattened shape. Put your present inside, and tape your box shut.

Tetrahedral puzzlers

These two brain-teasers are sometimes sold in gift shops, but you can make them yourself, following these instructions.

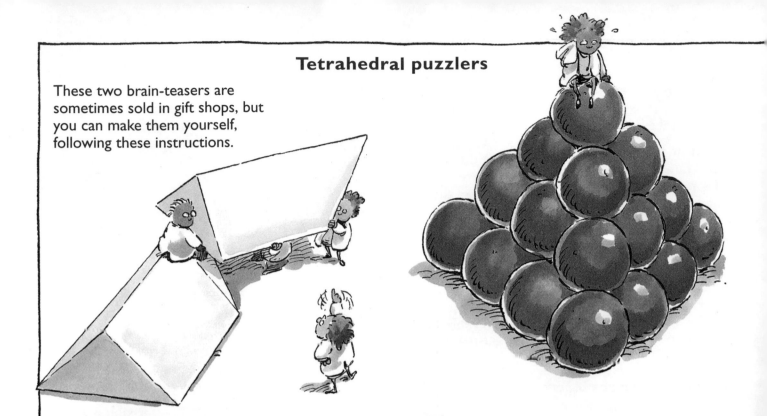

Tetrahedron match-up

It's harder than you might think to match up these two identical puzzle pieces to form a tetrahedron.

You'll need:
Bristol board
a ruler
a pencil
a compass
scissors
sticky tape

1. Construct an equilateral triangle with sides of 12 cm (6 inches) — see "Dissection puzzle" on page 30 for instructions on how to draw an equilateral triangle using a compass.

2. Measure the sides with your ruler, and mark the points that divide the sides into thirds — each segment will be 4 cm (2 inches). Make your measurements as exact as possible, so that the edges of the puzzle piece will fit together neatly later.

3. Construct a square on the middle segment of one side. (Squares have sides that are all the same length and right angles of 90°.)

4. Draw four lines as shown to join the division points you have marked on the sides of the equilateral triangle.

5. Use the ruler and the point of the compass to score the lines inside the shape. Scoring the lines makes the cardboard easier to fold.

6. Cut out the shape you have drawn, which should look a bit like a Christmas tree. Cut off the small triangle on the top.

7. Fold along the scored lines. Tape the sides together to finish the puzzle piece.

8. Make a second puzzle piece, exactly the same as the first one.

Now comes the tricky part. Can you fit these pieces fit together to make a tetrahedron? Give up? (See page 64 for the answer.)

Grape puzzle

The challenge in this puzzle is to stack 20 spheres so that they form a tetrahedron.

You'll need:

20 seedless grapes, all the same size (you could use Plasticine balls instead)
6 wooden toothpicks

1. Put four grapes on a toothpick as shown. Break off the extra length of toothpick.

2. Repeat step 1 so that you have two columns of four grapes.

3. Put three grapes on a toothpick. Break off the extra length of toothpick.

4. Repeat step 3 three more times so that you have four columns of three grapes.

5. Arrange these six columns to make a tetrahedron. (See page 64 for the answer.)

Here's a hint. Each face of the tetrahedron will look like this.

Bucky building

When the great American architect Buckminster Fuller was in kindergarten in 1899, his teacher asked the class to try using toothpicks and peas to make houses. Everyone made cubes—everyone except for Bucky. He fitted his peas and toothpicks together into triangles. Then he combined his triangles into tetrahedra and octahedra, which he could put together to fill up space without leaving any gaps. His teacher was so amazed by his space-filling triangles that she called in another teacher to admire them.

Why didn't Bucky make rectangular houses, just like everyone else? It turned out that he was almost blind, and had never clearly seen the rectangular world around him, where walls and ceilings meet at right angles. So he used his sense of touch, discovering for himself how triangles hold their shape and make solid structures. Fifty years later, he became world-famous for designs based on what he called the octet truss—the same shape he had discovered in his kindergarten classroom.

Unlike cubes, tetrahedra won't pack together to fill space without leaving gaps in between. Packing tetrahedra is more like packing marbles, where air-holes are left in between. But if you use octahedra and tetrahedra together, you can completely fill space. Buckminster Fuller called this shape, combining octahedra and tetrahedra, an octet truss.

Toothpick architecture

1. At least five hours before you want to start building, put 75 mL (1/4 cup) of dried peas in the bowl, cover them with water and set them aside to soak. You can start soaking the peas the night before you want to use them. But don't leave them soaking for two or three days, or they will start to sprout.

2. When you are ready to start building, poke the ends of the toothpicks into the peas as shown. With three peas and three toothpicks, you can make a triangle. Add one more pea and three more sticks and you have a tetrahedron.

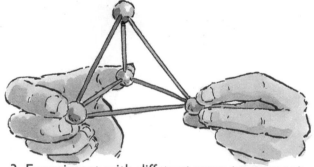

3. Experiment with different ways to connect toothpicks to make towers and buildings.

4. Put your creations on a shelf to dry. After a day or two, the peas dry out and shrink and then will hold the toothpicks securely.

Check out for yourself Buckminster Fuller's theories on building with triangles. Make your own toothpick architecture, and compare the shape-holding power of triangles and squares.

You'll need:
a bowl
water
some dried peas (whole peas, not split peas)
a box of round, cocktail toothpicks. The
  toothpicks should be pointed on each end. (Use
  coloured toothpicks to make
  your creations more fun.)

Alexander Graham Bell and the tetrahedron

Long before Buckminster Fuller was singing the praises of the tetrahedron, Alexander Graham Bell, the inventor of the telephone, was building them—hundreds of them. He made windbreaks, kites and cabins from tetrahedra. You might think a tetrahedron would be a good shape for a cabin because there would be so few walls to build—only four. Alexander Graham Bell and his wife seemed to find their cabin comfortable, but most people would find it too cramped inside. The tetrahedron has the least possible inside space in relation to its outside surface.

After Bell invented the telephone, he devoted

his time to inventing a flying machine. His dream was to build a kite that would carry a person into the air. Starting with a tetrahedrally shaped kite as a basic building block, he joined many small kites together to make giant ones. During his experiments, he made about 1200 tetrahedral kites. The biggest one, called the Cygnet, was made from 3393 tetrahedrally shaped cells. In 1907, this kite hoisted a man 50 m (165 feet) into the air. Some of Bell's experimental kites are in the Bell Museum on Cape Breton Island in Nova Scotia, Canada. This museum was built featuring—guess what shape—the triangle, of course!

6 Pyramids

The sides of a pyramid all meet at one point called the vertex. This means that its top half is much smaller and lighter than its bottom half. When a pyramid is sitting on its base, it's like this bottle of salad dressing — very stable because most of its weight is below the midpoint. (Of course, if you stand the bottle on its top, the slightest shake will make it topple over.)

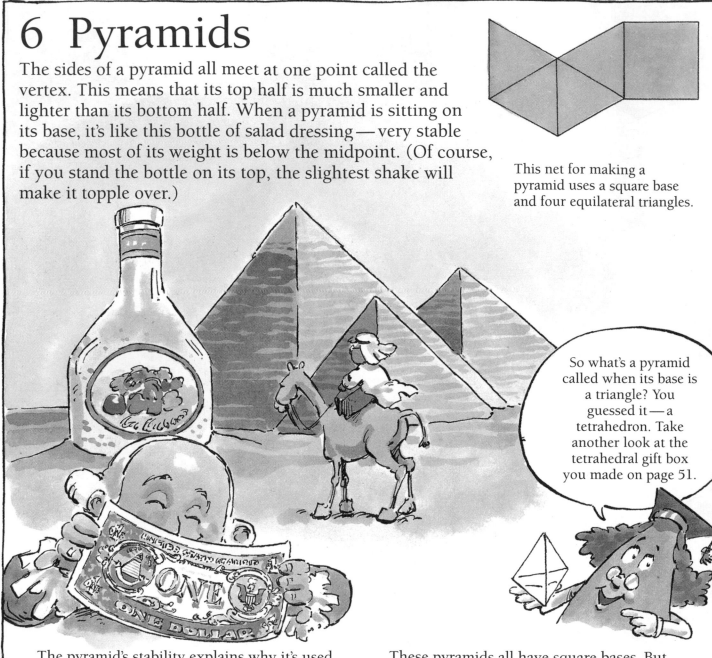

This net for making a pyramid uses a square base and four equilateral triangles.

So what's a pyramid called when its base is a triangle? You guessed it — a tetrahedron. Take another look at the tetrahedral gift box you made on page 51.

The pyramid's stability explains why it's used for monuments that are intended to last forever. The ancient Egyptians built mud huts to live in themselves. But for their Pharaohs' tombs, which were to house the souls of the dead throughout eternity, they built pyramids of stone. When Americans wanted a symbol of stability and eternity for their one-dollar bill, they chose a picture of a stone pyramid.

These pyramids all have square bases. But pyramids can also have bases that are triangles, pentagons, hexagons and so on. They are still pyramids as long as they have sides that are triangles meeting at one point. How many faces will a pyramid have? That's easy — the same number of faces as the number of sides in its base.

Leonardo's parachute

Pyramids don't all have to be as heavy as stone. In 1485, Leonardo da Vinci, the great Italian sculptor, painter and inventor, designed this lightweight pyramid as a parachute.

Make a pyramid

Experiment with pyramids of different bases.

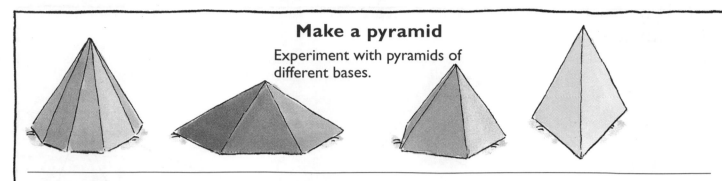

You'll need:

Bristol board or cardboard
a compass
a pencil
a ruler
scissors
glue

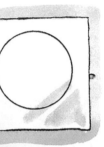

1. Use your compass to draw a circle on the Bristol board.

2. Keep the same compass opening that you used for the circle. Mark a point anywhere on the outside of the circle. Put the compass foot on this point and draw an arc to intersect the circle at a second point.

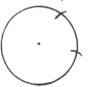

3. Continue around the circle in the same way, using your compass to draw four more division points. You have now divided the circle into six equal parts.

4. Use your ruler to draw six equilateral triangles connecting the centre of the circle and the division points.

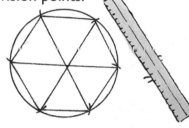

5. Cut out the hexagon.

6. Cut along one of the lines that connects a division point to the centre.

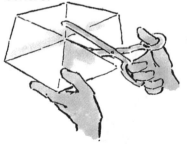

7. Using the pointed foot of the compass, score the other five lines. Fold along the lines.

8. Experiment with pyramids with different-shaped bases. Overlap one of the triangular faces to make a five-sided pyramid. Overlap three faces to get a tetrahedron. Finally overlap two faces to make a square-based pyramid. Glue the two overlapping faces together.

Volume of a square pyramid

Turn the square-based pyramid upside-down. If you filled this hollow container with water, how many containersful would it take to fill up a square prism with the same base and height? (See page 64 for the answer.)

The Egyptian pyramids

The Great Pyramid is one of the Seven Wonders of the World, as silent and mysterious today as when it was first built 4500 years ago. It's the largest of three pyramids at Giza on the river Nile. It was made from more than 2 million stone blocks weighing 2.3 metric tons each, and it covers an area the size of ten city blocks. Why build such a gigantic monument? The Great Pyramid was a royal tomb for the Pharaoh Khufu. But some Egyptologists think it may also have been a gigantic public works program to give jobs to Egyptian farmers while the Nile was flooding their lands each fall. Others think it served as a temple for the Sun-god Re. It does seem to have been built as a gigantic astrological instrument for watching the sun and stars and for establishing true north. It can't be just a coincidence that the four corners of the pyramid's square base are like a compass pointing exactly to the north, south, east and west.

At the centre of the Great Pyramid were the Pharoah's burial chambers. These chambers could be reached by a steeply climbing corridor 47 m (153 feet) long. After Khufu's funeral, huge granite blocks were slid down this passageway to close off the burial chambers and protect the golden treasures buried with him. But even Egyptian engineering genius couldn't keep out robbers, who broke into the burial chambers and stole the treasures inside.

Aztec pyramids

The Indians of Central and South America also built colossal pyramids. The Pyramid of the Sun, near present-day Mexico City, once formed the centre of a great civilization that flourished about 1500 years ago. This pyramid has two giant staircases on the north and south walls that lead to a sanctuary on the top.

Glossary

Acute angle an angle that is less than 90°

Altitude a line from any vertex that is at right angles, or perpendicular, to the opposite side

Angle the V-shape formed by two straight lines that intersect at a common point

Base usually the lowest side of a triangle

Bisect to divide into two equal parts

Congruent having the same size and shape

Degree a unit used to measure angles

Edge a line segment formed where two faces of a solid meet

Equilateral triangle a triangle having three sides of equal length

Face any flat side that makes up a solid figure

Geometry the study of the shape and size of things

Hypotenuse the side across from the right angle in a right triangle

Intersect to share at least one point in common. For example, two straight lines can intersect at a common point.

Isosceles triangle a triangle having two sides of equal length

Median of a triangle a line from any vertex of a triangle to the midpoint of the opposite side

Midpoint the point that divides a line into two equal parts

Obtuse angle an angle greater than 90° and less than 180°

Parallel lines two lines in the same plane that are an equal distance apart

Parallelogram a closed, four-sided figure having opposite sides parallel

Polygon a closed, flat shape made of straight lines

Polyhedron a closed, solid shape having polygonal faces, such as a cube or a tetrahedron

Regular polygon a polygon having all sides the same length and all interior angles the same size

Right angle an angle of 90°, such as this book's corner

Scalene triangle a triangle in which each side is a different length

Similar triangles triangles that are the same shape, but not necessarily the same size

Solid a three-dimensional figure, such as a tetrahedron, pyramid, cube or sphere

Symmetry repetition of exactly alike parts either on opposite sides of a line or rotated around a central point

Triangulation the use of a network of triangles to survey and map out a piece of land

Vertex a point where two sides of a triangle meet

Volume the amount of space inside a solid

Triangle formulas

The **perimeter** of a triangle is the sum of the length of its sides.

The **area** of a triangle is 1/2 bh (1/2 length of base × height).

The **volume** of a square-based pyramid is 1/3 Ah (1/3 area of base × height).

Pythagorean theorem: In a right-angled triangle, the square formed on the hypotenuse is equal to the sum of the squares formed on the other sides.

Index

Answers

Find the hidden triangles, page 9.
There are 44 triangles—16 small triangles, 16 triangles made of 2 small triangles, 8 triangles made of 4 small triangles and 4 big triangles made of 8 small triangles.

Pascal's triangle, page 15.
The next row in Pascal's triangle is:
1   8   28   56   70   56   28   8   1

Turn the triangle around, page 15.
You have to move three pennies. Move the pennies at the vertexes clockwise as shown.

Triangle take-away, page 17.

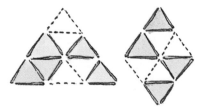

Tetrahedron match-up, pages 52-53.
Match the two square faces together. If necessary, give one of the pieces a 90° turn. As you can see, one of the cross-sections of a tetrahedron is a square.

Grape puzzle, page 53.
Arrange the columns as shown.

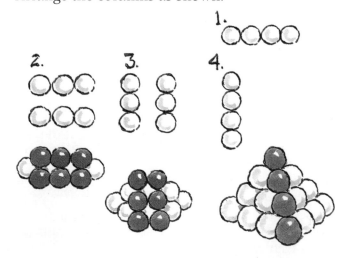

Volume of a square pyramid, page 60.
It would take three square pyramids to fill a square prism. The volume of a square pyramid is one-third the volume of a square prism with the same base and height.